Ese cuerpo no soy

I Am Not That Body

Ese cuerpo no soy

I Am Not That Body

Verónica González Arredondo

Trans. Allison A. deFreese

Pub House Books · Montreal

FIRST PUB HOUSE BOOKS EDITION, JUNE 2020

I Am Not That Body
Copyright © 2020 by Verónica González Arredondo
Translation copyright © 2020 by Allison A. deFreese

The Spanish language poems in this chapbook were previously published by Universidad Autónoma de Zacatecas, 2015. The English translations of "Mamá, what is that in the distance, far out at sea?" and "Epitaph" first appeared in *Waxwing* (Issue XX, 2020); "I Am Not That Body" first appeared in *Aymptote*. Grateful acknowledgement is made to the editors.

Library and Archives Canada Cataloguing in Publication

Title: Ese cuerpo no soy = I am not that body / Verónica González Arredondo ; trans. Allison A.
  deFreese.
Other titles: I am not that body
Names: González Arredondo, Verónica, author. | DeFreese, Allison A., 1973- translator. | container
  of (work): González Arredondo, Verónica. Ese cuerpo no soy. | container of (expression):
  González Arredondo, Verónica. Ese cuerpo no soy. English.
Description: Pub House Books edition. | Poems. | Poems in English and Spanish; translated from the
  Spanish.
Identifiers: Canadiana 20200213180 | ISBN 9781989266250 (softcover)
Classification: LCC PQ7298.417.O59 E8413 2020 | DDC 861/.7—dc23

ISBN-13 978-1-989266-25-0

Poetry translated by Allison A. deFreese
Edited and facilitated by Andrew Lafleche
Cover image "Nocturnal Calls" © by Sophia Forrester

Pub House Books
1918 Boul. Saint-Regis
Dorval, QC H9P 1H6
www.pubhousebooks.com

Printed in the United States of America

Translator's Notes

In her succinct, richly imagistic poetry, Verónica González Arredondo explores the arid desert ecosystems in which she spent her childhood, as well as themes related to: immigration, social justice, femicide, perilous border crossings, and the vanishings of countless girls and women in northern Mexico who were making the journey across harsh terrain toward the United States border. She writes about extinction and survival, disappearing landscapes, displaced peoples, and the inhospitable climate—physically and politically—that remain in their wake. Her work merits consideration for publication in English today, more than ever, considering the devastating impact of current U.S. border policies on immigrant children, women and families.

Although her books have previously been translated into French and Portuguese, *I Am Not That Body,* is the first time her work has been translated into English.

Ese cuerpo no soy

I Am Not That Body

a mi madre

to my mother

Algo le duele al aire,
del aroma al hedor [...]
entre las altas frondas
de los árboles altos [...]
de cuanto él se duele
algo me duele a mí,
algo me duele.

—Dolores Castro

Something pains the wind [. . .]
and something hurts me
as much as the wind hurts,
something hurts me,
something hurts me.

—Dolores Castro

PRIMAVERA EN EL ÁRTICO

> *Yo te escribo desde donde todo camino es hacia abajo.*
> *Yo te escribo entrando en una fosa para venir a verte.*
>
> *—Dolores Dorantes*

humedad en el lugar donde era mi boca

afuera es agosto

llueve

y ni siquiera lirios han crecido en este pantano

si tan sólo pudieran sabernos
bajo los lirios de un agosto incierto
bajo la sal entera del mar
bajo el pantano de nuestra sangre rumiando raíces

aquí

SPRING IN THE ARCTIC

> I write you from a place where all paths lead downward.
> As I write you, I am entering a grave to come and see you.
>
> —Dolores Dorantes

dampness
in the place that was my mouth

outside it is August

and raining

not even lilies
have grown in this swamp

if only they knew we were here,
beneath the lily beds of this uncertain August
beneath all the salt in the sea
beneath the swamp
of our own blood
chewing on the roots

                                        here

aquellas piernas
las de la mujer que mira fijamente
recuerdan la primavera en el Ártico
un lago circundado de flores amarillas
bajo el agua sus pies
el hielo subiéndole por los huesos
aquellas piernas
aquel rostro
tan parecido al mío

those legs
the ones belonging to the woman with the fixed stare
bring to mind spring in the Arctic,
a lake surrounded by yellow flowers
her feet underwater
as the ice rises over her bones
those legs
that face
so similar to my own

ante el encuentro fortuito entre la luz del amanecer

y la germinación interminable de lirios
esta voz desconoce nombrar
como aparición
y desnombrar
como desapariciones

at a chance encounter between daybreak

and the interminable germination of lilies,
this voice does not know how to name—
an *appearance*—
or to unname—
a *disappearance*

a esta mujer le hiere el agua y el amarillo

aquella
y su visceral abrazo (interminable)
otra
tiene un lirio en los ojos

debería hervir una cruz en medio de nada
una señal en la llanura
aquí yace un jardín hibernal
pétalos amarillos resplandecen con terror
  de glaciares
al fondo de un lago

the water and yellow flowers

are hurting this woman,
and another
with her (endless) visceral embrace
and yet another
whose eyes have a lily inside them

a cross should be boiled in the middle of nowhere,
a sign on this flat expanse:
here lies a winter garden
where yellow petals sparkle with the terror
        of glaciers
at the bottom of a lake

pido al vendaval se apiade de mis huesos pulidos
     con el filo de su aliento
apilados se levantan de la tierra en cadenas
     montañosas
cordillera de fríos incendios
tan blanca

hay quienes piden huesos
almohadas para llorar

I ask the sharp wind
    with the blade in its breath
to please take pity on my polished bones—
stacked in piles, they rise from the earth
in mountainous
    chains
a range of cold fires, so very white

there are those who ask for bones
to use as pillows to cry on

AL AIRE EL CUERPO DUELE

Frontera: desierto/mar

Yo tampoco escogí venir a esta playa de cactáceas
    y luciérnagas voraces

ni escogí andar descalza con la aridez rasgando
    mi rostro

En este desierto de flor inmarcesible
todo yace aquí fosilizado

Atrapaba estrellas fugaces
y piedras para lanzar al infinito

Yo no quería venir a este matadero
donde cuerpos navegan bajo tierra o boca abajo
    en el mar
La playa es un paso en falso:
      al fondo
    una fila de rocas

Dirán que fue suicidio

THE BODY PAINS THE WIND

Border: Desert/Ocean

I didn't choose to come here to this beach of cacti
    and ravenous fireflies;

I didn't ask to walk barefoot with the dryness scratching
    at my face

Everything lies fossilized here
in this desert where stone flowers never whither.

I was catching falling stars,
collecting pebbles
    to throw into infinity

I didn't want to come to this slaughterhouse
where bodies are sailing along underground,
    or float facedown in the sea

The beach is another misstep:
    in the depths of its water
    a row of rocks

They will say it was suicide.

Me arrebataron de la tierra sin ser mi tiempo
Alguien vino hacía mí con la marea violenta
penetrándome cada costa del cuerpo

Alguien me dejó por pezones dos caracolas abiertas

De este mar sangre de mi sangre
vuela un pájaro esquelético
a postrarse en el corazón
        de los míos
Esperaré despierta con el rumor del aleteo en cada
        Piedra

Alguien: cuando los alacranes me suban por las piernas
quizás encuentren tu torso mutilado en la arena

They snatched me up from the earth
before *my time*
Someone approached me with the violent tide,
entering every inlet of my body

Someone left me two open conch shells for nipples

From this sea of my own flesh and blood
the skeleton of a bird takes flight
to lie prostrate in the heart
    of my beloveds
And I will lie awake, listening for the whisper of its wings in every
    stone

I say:
Someone,
when the scorpions climb up my legs
perhaps they will find your mutilated torso in the sand

Mamá, ¿qué es eso a lo lejos en el mar?

*Me he preguntado a menudo si era más fácil averiguar
la profundidad del océano o la profundidad del corazón humano.
Viejo océano...Tienes que decírmelo para que me alegre
al saber que el infierno está tan cerca del hombre.*

—Lautréamont

*Mamá, ¿qué es eso a lo lejos en el mar? Hay un animal que
duerme el sueño del océano: es ciego, tiene la piel viscosa, su boca
guarda hileras interminables de colmillos y, cuando bosteza,
devora los astros. ¿Y a qué hora bosteza? Cuando se oculta el sol.
No puede tragar fuego sin quemarse, por eso abre tan grande la
boca y lo oscurece todo. Encerrado, el sol grita, pero nosotras sólo
vemos las estrellas.*

Mama, what is that in the distance, far out at sea?

> I have often asked myself
> if it is easier to sound the ocean's depths
> or to fathom the depth of the human heart.
> Old ocean . . . You must tell me the answer,
> for I would be happy to know
> that hell is as near as man.
>
> —Lautréamont

Mama, what is that, far out at sea? An animal that falls asleep in the ocean's dream: It is blind; with viscous skin, and in its mouth—endless rows of fangs. When it yawns, it devours the heavens. And when does it yawn? When the sun sets. It can't swallow fire without burning itself; that's why when it opens its mouth so very wide, it makes the whole world go dark. Once trapped, the sun screams, but you and I see only stars.

Mamá ¿y qué es lo que está a lo lejos, lo que se ve desde aquí? Es una isla de cruces. ¿Quién las lleva hasta allá? La marea y el viento las llevan en una barca, una por cada niña o cada mujer. ¿Cómo saben que ellas no volverán? Unas están muertas en vida. Otras, cuando la playa está picada, tropiezan y se ahogan. El mar las golpea contra el acantilado hasta destrozarlas. Y yo de cuales soy: ¿de las que tropezaron o de las que mueren en vida?

And Mama, what is it we can see from here, that thing far out in the distance? It's an island filled with crosses. How do they get there? The tide and wind carry them over on a boat, one for every girl and every woman. How do they know the girls and women will never return? Some are already among the living dead. When the water is choppy, others fall in and drown. The sea smashes them against the cliffs until they break apart into nothing. And me? Which kind am I? The kind who stumbles and falls in, or the kind who is dead while still living?

Epitafio

Dejan una a la vez, en cada visita. Descalza de pies, desraizada. Doncella con vestido de pétalos, multicolor. Sobre esta lápida una joven releva el cuerpo derruido de otra. Ignoran que, recién cortadas, el proceso será inminente, como hueco en un reloj de arena, acelerando el viaje al siempre otoño. Una más y otra, en cada visita.

Epitaph

They leave them, one by one, one on every trip. Barefoot, uprooted: a damsel in a dress of multicoloured petals. At this grave site, one young woman takes the place of another's wrecked body. Freshly cut, they are unaware that the next step is imminent, just as the opening into the pit of an hourglass accelerates the sands' journey toward a never-ending autumn. One and then another, one more every trip.

Caracola abierta

mudar de nombre bajo la tierra

llamarme desde otra piel

al aire el cuerpo duele

busca la lengua del eco

que me arrastra a esta voz

Open Seashell

to change names underground

to call out to myself

from within a different skin

the body pains the wind,

seeking the tongue of echoes,

dragging me toward this voice

LA BESTIA

Cruza el territorio a 160 km/hr
es el rastro de un dedo índice pinchado
una máquina programada para devorar y transportar
su aliento lacera el cuerpo
y quienes rozan su vientre desde el ángulo impreciso
caen invariablemente en una fosa común

THE BEAST

It cuts across the land at 100 mph
leaving behind traces of blood
like a punctured finger—
a machine programmed to transport and devour
its breath lacerates the body
and those who brush against its belly at the wrong angle
invariably fall into a common grave

Fue un calor repentino
el alargado vientre del ciempiés metálico
cruzó interminable sobre mis ojos
me levanté sin brazos ni piernas
la que fui quedó esparcida en las vías
incluso el llanto

There was a sudden heat
when the elongated belly
of the metal centipede
made its endless journey over my eyes

I arose without arms or legs
the pieces that had been me
lay scattered on the tracks
even my cry

La bestia me jaló por los pies
aferrada a mis uñas
trepada en su lomo
me dijeron:
no duermas
pero nadie dijo:
no sueñes

recordé a mi padre
él jugaba a ser mi caballo
y yo a ser el viento con mi cabello
sonreíamos
aquel vaivén no podía ser otra cosa que la felicidad

el triturador de vísceras me jaló por los pies
como la bruja

The Beast dragged me by my feet—
clinging with my fingernails
I climbed onto its flank
don't sleep,
they told me,
but no one ever said:
don't dream

I remembered my father
pretending he was my horse
as I pretended I was the wind in my hair

we were both smiling
that rocking back and forth
could only have been happiness

the meat grinder dragged me by the feet
like a witch

Estancias en el extranjero

Se ha borrado la línea entre el desierto y mi cuerpo

Frontera:
¿a dónde viaja?
Documentos:
pasaporte en mano
Identifíquese:
visitante, trabajadora fronteriza
Destino:

> *quiero volver a mi cuerpo*
> *llamar mi nombre*
> *habitarme*
> *sin otras lágrimas nuestras*

Visits Abroad

The line separating my body from the desert has been erased

The Border:
where are you travelling?
Documents:
my passport in hand
Identity:
visiting cross-border worker
Destination:

> I want to return to my body
> to call out my own name
> and to live inside myself
> without any more of our tears

Nombre:
la que sé que no soy
y me vuelvo
Ciudad de origen:
Guatemala
mis piernas
mi patria

Identificación:
con los ojos aterrados por ser reconocida
estoy
en todas partes
de la ausencia

Pase de abordar:
aquí
me disuelvo

No importa dónde estemos
renaceré para nombrar el mar
A pan y agua este vuelo se abrió para nosotras
este vuelo
no la pertenencia

Name:
Someone I know isn't me
so I'm returning again
Place of origin:
Guatemala City
my legs
my homeland

Identification:
with these eyes terrified of being recognized
I am
everywhere
where there is absence

Boarding pass:
and this is where
I dissolve

No matter where we may be
I will be reborn to name the sea,
With rations of bread and the water
this flight opened for us
this flight
but not a sense of belonging

El vuelo de un pájaro autómata desciende
Cierro los ojosAlarma de extravío
luces rojas
El calor repentino me invade
fragmenta mis huesos

Destino final:
el fuego

The robotic bird in flight descends
I close my eyes
at the alarm of going astray
flashing red lights
The sudden heat
overwhelms me
splintering my bones

Final destination:
the fire

ESE CUERPO NO SOY

Cuando la noche bosteza
hay en su boca hileras de dientes
que penetran cada hueso de la tierra

I AM NOT THAT BODY

When the night yawns
there are rows of teeth in its mouth
that pierce every bone in the earth

Cubre mi boca la violencia de un pañuelo blanco
no grito
no respiro
todos mis recuerdos perderán su lengua
seré otra
idéntica a la voz que ya jamás reconocí

grito para despertar en otro sueño
pero el sueño es extravío

The violence of a white handkerchief covers my mouth
I don't scream
I don't breathe
all my memories
will lose their tongue
I will become another,
identical to the voice I never recognized

I scream in order to wake up in another dream
but the dream has gone missing

Por la calle veías el charco de sangre
        bajo la puerta
        mientras caminabas
antes de levantar los cuerpos
ya saben quiénes fueron
uno recibe la llamada:
Las dejamos tumbadas en el borde
y cuando llegues
ya sabes qué hacer.

You saw the pool of blood
    on the street
    in the doorway
    as you were out walking—
before the bodies were carried away
they already know
who was responsible—
the call comes in:
We left them lying by the side of the road
and when you get there—
you know what to do.

La quinceañera
enterrada en el desierto
en ceremonia comunitaria
tomadas de la mano las mujeres recuerdan
a otras jovencitas
que habitan el cielo pintado de rosa
con una cruz enlutada

The *quinceañera,*
buried in the desert at 15
during a community ceremony—
the women hold hands, remembering
the other girls
who live in a sky
painted pink
by a cross decked in mourning

Santa María Madre ruega por ellas
y por nosotras
aquí no hay nadie
ni Dios que mire
en el séptimo día
con sus manos cuervo
sacó sus ojos
danos paz

Mother Santa Maria, pray for them
and for us,
here no one
is watching, not even God—
on the seventh day
with his crow hands
he plucked out his own eyes
give us peace

El camposanto está rodeado de signos:
sin cruces
flores
ni plegarias entre la basura
al epitafio lo acompaña
una hija de Dios
no
identificada

The cemetery is surrounded by signs:
no crosses
no flowers
no prayers lying scattered in the trash
the epitaph accompanied
daughter of God
unidentified

Confundieron a mi familia
con un cráneo sin orejas
sin nariz
ni labios para decir

madre
padre
ese cuerpo
no soy

They baffled my family
with a skull that had no ears,
no nose,
no lips that could say

mother
father
I am not
that body

Verónica González Arredondo

Biography

Verónica González Arredondo (Guanajuato, Mexico) holds a PhD in Arts from the Universidad de Guanajuato and a Master's in Philosophy from the Universidad de Zacatecas. She has received several prestigious Latin American literary awards, including Mexico's National Ramón López Velarde Prize in Poetry/Premio Nacional de Poesía "Ramón López Velarde," for her book of poems Ese cuerpo no soy/I Am Not That Body (Universidad Autónoma de Zacatecas, 2015) as well as the Dolores Castro Prize in Poetry /Premio Dolores Castro en Poesía, an annual prize awarded to a woman writing exceptional and socially conscious work in Spanish, for her book Verde Fuegos de Espíritus/Green Fires of the Spirits (Ayuntamiento de Aguascalientes, 2014). Voracidad, grito y belleza animal/Voraciousness, Screams and Animal Beauty, a book of essays, was also published by Universidad Autónoma de Zacatecas in 2014. Verónica González Arredondo's books of verse have previously been translated into, and published in, French and Portuguese. From 2017-2018 she held a FONCA fellowship for younger artists through the Fondo Nacional para la Culturas y las Artes/National Fund for Arts and Culture.

Collaborators

Allison A. deFreese (Translator) is a literary translator and poet. She has lived in Mexico and Bolivia. Her work has appeared in *Waxwing, Crazyhorse, New York Quarterly, Anomaly,* and *Asymptote.* Her book-length translations forthcoming in 2020 include: María Negroni's genre-bending books *Elegy for Joseph Cornell* and *The Dickinson Archive,* and *Soaring to New Heights,* the autobiography of NASA astronaut and former child migrant farmworker José Moreno Hernández. Allison A. deFreese holds a BA from Ottawa University, an MFA in Poetry and Playwriting from the University of Texas at Austin, and an MA in Spanish Translation from the University of Texas at Brownsville (now UTRGV).

Sophia Forrester (Cover image artist) is a high school senior from Washington, D.C.

Andrew Lafleche (Volume editor, design) is an award-winning poet and the author of *Ashes, No Diplomacy, Shameless, A Pardonable Offence, One Hundred Little Victories, On Writing, Merica, Merica, on the Wall, After I Turn into Alcohol,* and *Ride.* He is editor of Gravitas Poetry. Lafleche received an M.A. in Creative and Critical Writing from the University of Gloucestershire. He lives in the Ottawa Valley. Visit AndrewLafleche.com or follow @AndrewLafleche on Twitter for more information.

www.ingramcontent.com/pod-product-compliance
Lightning Source LLC
Chambersburg PA
CBHW021942040426
42448CB00008B/1191